The 1963 Civil Rights March

Scott Ingram

WORLD ALMANAC® LIBRARY

Please visit our web site at: www.worldalmaclibrary.com
For a free color catalog describing World Almanac® Library's list of high-quality
books and multimedia programs, call 1-800-848-2928 (USA) or 1-800-387-3178
(Canada). World Almanac® Library's fax: (414) 332-3567.

Library of Congress Cataloging-in-Publication Data

Ingram, Scott.
    The 1963 civil rights march / by Scott Ingram.
      p. cm. — (Landmark events in American history)
    Includes bibliographical references and index.
    ISBN 0-8368-5392-X (lib. bdg.)
    ISBN 0-8368-5420-9 (softcover)
    1. March on Washington for Jobs and Freedom, Washington, D.C., 1963—Juvenile
literature. 2. Civil rights demonstrations—Washington (D.C.)—History—20th
century—Juvenile literature. 3. African Americans—Civil rights—Juvenile literature.
I. Title. II. Series.
    F200.I54   2004
    323.1196'073'009046—dc22   2004042025

First published in 2005 by
World Almanac® Library
330 West Olive Street, Suite 100
Milwaukee, WI 53212 USA

Copyright © 2005 by World Almanac® Library.

Produced by Discovery Books
Editor: Sabrina Crewe
Designer and page production: Sabine Beaupré
Photo researcher: Sabrina Crewe
Maps and diagrams: Stefan Chabluk
World Almanac® Library editorial direction: Mark J. Sachner
World Almanac® Library editor: Jenette Donovan Guntly
World Almanac® Library art direction: Tammy West
World Almanac® Library production: Jessica Morris

Photo credits: Corbis: cover, pp. 4, 5, 7, 9, 10, 13, 15, 19, 20, 21, 25, 27, 28, 29, 30, 31,
32, 33, 34, 35, 36, 37, 38, 42, 43; Library of Congress: 6, 8, 11, 12, 14, 16, 17, 18, 22,
23, 24, 39, 40, 41.

Printed in Canada

1 2 3 4 5 6 7 8 9 08 07 06 05 04

Contents

Introduction   4

Chapter 1: From Slavery to Segregation   6

Chapter 2: The Civil Rights Movement   14

Chapter 3: Planning the March   22

Chapter 4: A Day in Washington, D.C.   28

Chapter 5: New Voices of Protest   38

Conclusion   42

Time Line   44

Glossary   45

Further Information   46

Index   47

Introduction

Thousands of marchers assembled at the Washington Monument, seen in the background here. They then marched to the Lincoln Memorial about 1 mile (1.6 kilometers) away.

A Gentle Army

"No one could remember an invading army quite as gentle as the two hundred thousand civil-rights marchers who occupied Washington today. . . . The sweetness and patience of the crowd may have set some sort of national high-water mark in mass decency."

Russell Baker, describing the march, the New York Times, *August 1963*

The March on Washington

Washington, D.C., was filled with more than 200,000 extra Americans on Wednesday, August 28, 1963. People from around the country had come to the nation's capital to take part in the March on Washington for Jobs and Freedom. The marchers began arriving early on the day of the march. They came in trains and planes, by bus and by car.

After gathering in the center of the city, the marchers listened to speeches. Those speeches included one by Martin Luther King, Jr., who gave what is now considered one of the greatest orations in American history.

The 1963 March on Washington was a protest about **civil rights**. It was also the largest **demonstration** in U.S. history up to that time, and the event is still widely remembered as one of the most powerful, yet peaceful, demonstrations ever held in the nation's capital.

The Larger Struggle

The event took place a hundred years after President Abraham Lincoln made the **Emancipation** Proclamation, freeing slaves in the South. One hundred years had passed, but racial inequality was still present in U.S. society. The march was part of a larger struggle by black people to achieve basic rights in a nation founded on ideas of freedom and equality.

This struggle was called the civil rights movement, and it was at its height in the 1960s. Most historians agree that the 1963 march marked a key point in the movement because it was the point at which there was the greatest amount of white support for civil rights, as well as the highest level of hope among African Americans that the U.S. government would address inequality and **segregation** in the United States.

A statue of President Abraham Lincoln looks out across the Reflecting Pool in front of the Lincoln Memorial. The site was a fitting destination for civil rights marchers because Lincoln freed African Americans from slavery.

Making the Kingdom Real

"That day, for a moment, it almost seemed that we stood on a height, and could see our inheritance; perhaps we could make the kingdom real, perhaps the beloved community would not forever remain the dream one dreamed in agony."

Author James Baldwin, describing the day of the 1963 march

Chapter 1

From Slavery to Segregation

African Americans celebrated the banning of slavery in Washington, D.C., in 1862, a year before the Emancipation Proclamation declared freedom for slaves in southern states.

Lincoln Abolishes Slavery

While white Americans declared their independence in 1776, the first national declaration of freedom for African Americans did not take place until 1863. For about 250 years, African and African-American slaves had been bought and sold in the North American slave trade.

In 1863, President Abraham Lincoln issued the Emancipation Proclamation, declaring slaves in the southern states free. In 1865, the Thirteenth **Amendment** banned slavery throughout the United States. Former slaves, however, were free in name only.

New Kinds of Inequality

After slavery was outlawed, the **federal** government used laws, social programs, and the military to protect the rights of southern blacks. By the late 1870s, however, the federal government had abandoned the South to **racist** state governments. Whites in the

The Fourteenth Amendment

While the Thirteenth Amendment to the Constitution was important in that it ended slavery, the Fourteenth Amendment, passed by Congress in 1866—and finally approved in 1868—went a step further. Many historians consider it the most important amendment to the Constitution since the original Bill of Rights.

The first section of the amendment defines a citizen of the United States as anyone born or **naturalized** in the country. It gives all citizens the right to "equal protection under the law" and says that those rights cannot be taken away without "due process of law." This section extended to African Americans the benefits and protection given to all U.S. citizens.

South—where most former slaves lived—soon found new ways to deny the rights of African Americans.

Former soldiers, who had fought to retain slavery in the Civil War, began to form secret terrorist groups to intimidate blacks. The best known of these terrorist organizations was the Ku Klux Klan,

By the 1920s, the Ku Klux Klan had grown so powerful that it held a national rally and parade in Washington, D.C. The rally drew over fifty thousand marchers and a huge crowd of spectators.

but others, such as the Tennessee Pale Faces, the Red Jackets, and Knights of the Red Cross, were equally vicious. Thousands of blacks were driven from their homes, tortured, and **lynched**.

Jim Crow

Above all, it was segregation that kept the blacks from gaining equality. State laws in the South, called **Jim Crow** laws, made sure that blacks and whites went to separate schools, used separate public facilities, ate in separate restaurants, stayed in separate hotels, and more.

Local governments also passed laws allowing voting by only those citizens whose grandfathers had voted. Since the grandfathers of most blacks had been slaves—who were ineligible to vote—African Americans in the South gradually lost their political voice.

Segregation Takes Hold

By the beginning of the twentieth century, the South had two separate societies: black and white. Segregation spread widely across the South and to other states. Official segregation was supported by the unofficial use of terrorism

Like everything else in the South during the Jim Crow years, these drinking fountains at the county courthouse in Albany, Georgia, were segregated. Public facilities for black people were usually inferior to those for whites.

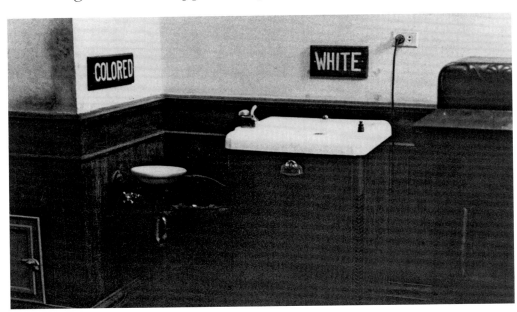

against African Americans. Lynching and other forms of racist violence helped to keep the power in the hands of white people, including lawmakers who favored Jim Crow laws.

Early Signs of Protest

Despite their lack of political power, African Americans developed organizations to fight segregation wherever possible. Most of the organizing took place in black churches, which provided safe gathering places. From these locations, black communities offered education, welfare, leadership training, and protest strategies.

Eventually, black and white Americans with similar religious and political beliefs formed a national organization to fight for civil rights. This group was the National Association for the Advancement of Colored People (NAACP), formed in 1909.

The NAACP

Founded in 1909, the NAACP was originally called the National Negro Committee. The organization was formed by early civil rights leaders, including W. E. B. Du Bois, who also edited its journal, the *Crisis*, for many years. The NAACP really grew in size and influence after the huge black migration to the North that started in 1914. For fifty years, the NAACP was the main organization in the fight for African-American civil rights. It achieved this position by defending individual African Americans

The NAACP headquarters in Detroit, Michigan, in the 1950s.

against social injustice, protesting racism, and continually pushing for **legislation** that would end racial violence and secure equal rights. Throughout the 1960s, the height of the civil rights movement, the NAACP was very active in nonviolent protest and **voter registration**. The NAACP is still fighting **discrimination** and promoting equal opportunities today.

Work in the North

Even with a national organization supporting the struggle, however, African Americans were targets of hatred and prejudice in the South. Thus, when industrial jobs in the North became available in 1914 at the beginning of World War I, millions of black Americans left their homes in the South to work in northern cities such as Chicago, Detroit, and New York City. This mass migration created enormous social change as northern cities developed large African-American communities.

Harlem in New York City, seen here in the 1920s, was one of several neighborhoods in northern cities that became African-American communities. People who migrated north after World War I found a prosperity and freedom they never would have achieved in southern states.

Lynching in the South

At the same time, most African Americans lived in the South under conditions that became even more segregated and brutal. Violence against blacks increased during the second and third decades of the twentieth century, when the Ku Klux Klan grew to more than 2 million members and spread to midwestern states.

As the Klan's numbers grew, so did its activities. Lynching became one of the most common forms of terror. In Georgia in the 1920s, for example, one African American was lynched every two days on average.

The NAACP sought to call attention to the horrors of lynching with this banner, hanging outside the organization's office in New York City. The banner was displayed every time a person was lynched.

During that decade, the NAACP attempted to get the U.S. Congress to pass several federal antilynching laws. Southern senators, however, opposed the laws. Murder was a state crime rather than a federal crime, they said. It was up to states to prevent the killings, not the federal government. The laws failed to pass.

The New Deal

Although the NAACP drew national attention in the 1920s with its efforts to get antilynching laws passed, African Americans had little actual influence on the federal government. In 1932, however, the election of Franklin D. Roosevelt changed the relationship between federal government and all citizens. During the Great Depression, Roosevelt introduced the "New Deal," a group of programs that created government-funded jobs for Americans. The NAACP used this opportunity to push for the inclusion of black people in government-sponsored programs.

New Deal programs and legislation altered race relations across the country. By 1935,

Seeing It Differently

"Segregation is not a humiliation but a benefit, and ought to be so regarded by you gentlemen."

President Woodrow Wilson, speaking to African-American federal workers, 1916

The Works Progress Administration (WPA), one of Roosevelt's New Deal programs, engaged in huge projects such as the construction of highways, bridges, and public buildings. These WPA workers were laboring on a construction project in the late 1930s.

black advisers in the federal government had created what was called the "Black Cabinet" to speak out for African-American rights. Roosevelt's second term saw the rise of new organizations dedicated to challenging Jim Crow laws.

The Defense Industry and World War II

Although black people achieved some gains during the 1930s, racial discrimination shut blacks out of jobs in the defense industry, which grew rapidly when World War II spread across Europe and the Pacific. Among those speaking out against labor discrimination was A. Philip Randolph, the president of the Sleeping Car Porters Association (a **union** of railroad workers). In 1940, Randolph joined leaders of other African-American organizations to urge Roosevelt to ban discrimination in the defense industry, which the president did in 1941.

The battle for racial equality was overshadowed when the United States entered World War II in 1941. The conflict turned

This fighter squadron was photographed after an air raid in Italy during World War II. The men were all graduates of the Tuskegee Institute in Alabama, a training ground for African-American pilots.

out to have enormous consequences for African Americans, however. Nearly 1 million African Americans served in the armed forces, and, as in World War I, black Southerners migrated to defense jobs in the North. Meanwhile, membership in the NAACP increased from 18,000 members in 1940 to almost 400,000 by the war's end in 1945. In 1948, Roosevelt's successor, President Harry S. Truman, under pressure from Randolph, abolished segregation in the military.

Progress

After World War II, African-American veterans commanded new respect among all Americans. This respect resulted in voting power. From 1944 to 1948, the NAACP registered thousands of voters across the South with the help of black army veterans. In Birmingham, Alabama, for example, black veterans marched in uniform to register to vote.

The late 1940s brought other changes in American racial attitudes. In 1947, Jackie Robinson became the first African American to play major league baseball when he took the field for the Brooklyn Dodgers. Robinson's quiet determination in the face of the jeering fans and dirty play by some racist ballplayers drew wide attention to the national sport and to the issue of segregation.

Chapter 2

The Civil Rights Movement

In a bid to challenge segregation in universities, these six hopeful students applied to the University of Oklahoma in 1948. Some of them were already academically qualified. One of the group, retired professor George McLaurin (top left), was allowed to enter the university after an appeal in the courts, but he had to sit outside both the library and the classrooms and eat in the cafeteria at a separate time from the white students.

Resistance to Integration

White resistance to black civil rights increased in the South when the U.S. Supreme Court ruled in the *Brown v. Board of Education of Topeka* case in 1954. The court's unanimous decision was that denying a black girl access to an all-white school in her neighborhood was **unconstitutional**. This groundbreaking ruling reversed the court's 1896 decision in *Plessy v. Ferguson*, which said that "separate but equal" facilities were acceptable.

A Question of Equality

"We come then to the question presented: Does segregation of children in public schools solely on the basis of race, even though the physical facilities and other "tangible" factors may be equal, deprive the children of the minority group of equal educational opportunities? We believe that it does."

From the U.S. Supreme Court's Brown v. Board of Education *decision, 1954*

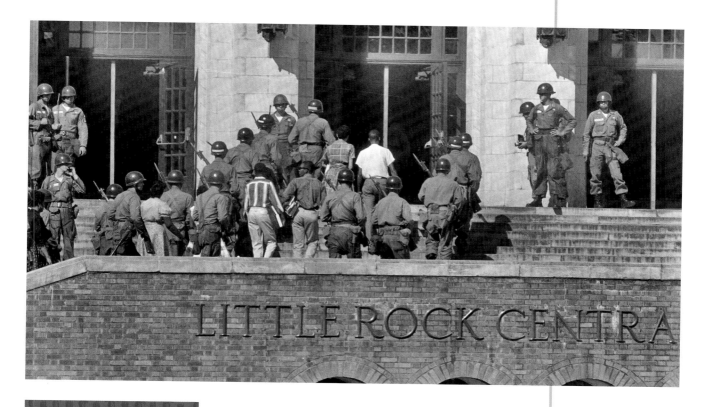

LITTLE ROCK CENTRA

The court, fearful of Southern white defiance, also issued an order that allowed for "all deliberate speed" to end segregation in schools. For most white Southerners, this meant they were allowed to resist **integration** for as long as possible. Over the next ten years, less than 2 percent of black children in the South attended white schools.

Little Rock

The resistance by southern leaders became apparent to the nation in the fall of 1957, when the Little Rock, Arkansas, school board attempted to integrate its high school. Governor Orval Faubus declared a state of emergency and sent in the National Guard to keep out black students. President Dwight Eisenhower responded to this action by sending about one thousand U.S. Army soldiers to Little Rock to escort the black children to school. The conflict over desegregating education continued into the 1960s.

African-American students were provided with military protection when they entered Little Rock Central High School in September 1957 during the desegregation of Arkansas public schools. In this photo, the African-American students are walking up the steps of the school entrance, flanked by soldiers.

15

In December 1956, after the U.S. Supreme Court ordered the desegregation of buses, Martin Luther King, Jr., (second row, left) took a ride on a Montgomery bus with a white colleague in the civil rights movement.

The Montgomery Bus Boycott

Meanwhile, the struggle was spreading into other areas. Public transportation had always been a target for segregationists. In 1955, Rosa Parks, an active NAACP member in Montgomery, Alabama, refused to surrender her seat on a city bus to a white man and move to the rear "colored" section. She was arrested for her refusal, and the attention of the civil rights movement turned to Montgomery.

To protest the segregation laws, the black community in the city **boycotted** the city buses. Hundreds of African Americans walked miles to work each day. Civil rights organizers in Montgomery elected Martin Luther King, Jr., a twenty-six-year-old local minister, to act as spokesperson for the boycott.

A New Leader Emerges

During the 381 days of the boycott, city leaders attempted to intimidate the boycott's leaders through arrests. King was jailed and his house was bombed. The nonviolent response by blacks in Montgomery to white anger, however, drew national and international attention to the cause. In late 1956, the U.S. Supreme Court prohibited segregation on the city's buses, and the boycott ended.

By that time, King was becoming widely known as an eloquent speaker for the civil rights movement. In 1957, he joined civil rights leaders Bayard Rustin and Ella Baker to create the Southern Christian Leadership Conference (SCLC). While the NAACP was involved in court battles to end discrimination on a national basis, the SCLC became the main organization for church-based, nonviolent protest groups across the South.

Endless Waiting

"For years now, I have heard the word 'Wait!' ring in the ear of every Negro with piercing familiarity. This 'Wait' has almost always meant 'Never.'"

Martin Luther King, Jr., Letter from a Birmingham Jail, 1963

16

Nonviolent Protest

In early 1960, the civil rights movement expanded into other areas of segregated society. A sit-in happens when people sit in a place and refuse to move as a protest. Civil rights protestors in the 1960s used sit-ins to protest laws that kept black people out of white restaurants, forced them to use separate drinking fountains and restrooms, and made them sit in separate areas at movie theaters and sporting events. The protestors at the sit-ins were mostly black, sitting in at whites-only facilities.

Sit-in protests spread across the South to many other segregated locations. In 1960, a number of young people who had participated in the sit-ins founded the

Making It Right

"This is my country. I fought for the chance to make it right."

Franklin McCain, one of the four students in the first lunch counter sit-in of 1960, interviewed in 1998

The Greensboro Sit-In

The first sit-in protest was in Greensboro, North Carolina, in 1960, when four students from Greensboro Agricultural and Technical College sat at the "whites-only" lunch counter in a local department store. The waitress refused to serve the students, and they sat at the lunch counter all day. The next day, twenty more students from the college, as well as white students from another local college,

Two of the students at the sit-in in Greensboro.

came to the sit-in. Angry whites poured food over the students, but they sat silently. By the fifth day of the sit-in, the original four had grown to hundreds. The sit-in continued for five months until the store owner agreed to serve black customers.

Another form of nonviolent protest is shown here. Members of the Student Nonviolent Coordinating Committee (SNCC) and the Congress of Racial Equality (CORE) chained themselves to a court-house to protest civil rights abuses in Mississippi.

Student Nonviolent Coordinating Committee (SNCC), another voice for civil rights at the local level.

Sit-ins were a good example of the kind of nonviolent protest adopted by the African-American civil rights movement of the 1950s and 1960s. The early civil rights **activists** were often church leaders, who believed fervently that everyone was equal in the eyes of God. They wanted to achieve equality through peaceful determination. Martin Luther King, for example, was an admirer of Mahatma Gandhi, who had led the people of India through many years of nonviolent action to achieve independence from British rule.

Marching in Birmingham

On the opposing side, however, violence against civil rights activists was common across the South. Few cities were more violent than Birmingham, Alabama. There, more than a dozen civil rights workers were killed. The SCLC believed that efforts to end segregation in Birmingham could draw widespread attention to the cause.

In April and May 1963, protestors marched to downtown Birmingham to protest segregation. By the beginning of May, there were over two thousand demonstrators in jail. The police did everything within their power to stop the marches. Violence came to a head when officers turned fire hoses on marchers, including children, and went after them with dogs. Nightly news broadcasts of the assault on peaceful protestors shocked the nation and the world.

The Power of Demonstrations

After several days of nonviolent response, blacks became enraged at the injuries inflicted on their community. Birmingham was at the edge of a race riot, and demonstrators were beginning to respond with violence despite the best efforts of the SCLC. To restore peace

CORE and the Freedom Riders

By spring 1961, another black civil rights group was staging protests: the Congress of Racial Equality (CORE), founded in 1942. CORE's leaders included Bayard Rustin, who later organized the March on Washington. The group wanted to force bus companies to obey a 1960 Supreme Court ruling banning segregation on interstate transportation. CORE also wanted to challenge the newly elected president, John F. Kennedy, to speak out for civil rights.

James Farmer, director of CORE, was one of the leaders of the 1963 March on Washington.

CORE called its protests "freedom rides." In a type of mobile sit-in, members rode buses from Washington, D.C., to the South. They refused to sit in designated racial areas on the bus or to use "colored" facilities in bus stations. In response, a bus was firebombed by segregationists outside Birmingham, Alabama. Another bus was invaded by a white mob at the bus station in Montgomery, Alabama. Throughout 1961 and into 1962, CORE continued to send freedom riders to protest on buses.

Demonstrators were slammed against buildings by the force of water from the hoses used by police in Birmingham in 1963. The protests were successful, however, and segregation laws were overturned in the city.

and help the city's reputation, local businesspeople agreed to desegregate downtown stores and employ black clerks. With federal troops stationed outside of the city, Birmingham's mayor agreed to repeal the city's segregation laws.

The Birmingham marches had shown the power of mass demonstrations. Soon, protest marches spread to cities across the South. The civil rights movement had gained national and international attention.

June 1963

By June 1963, the sit-ins, marches, and freedom rides had also gained the attention of President John F. Kennedy. Kennedy, however, was a Democrat and reluctant to upset the white southern Democrats in Congress because he needed their political support. Then, over three days in mid-June, events forced Kennedy to take action to support integration.

On June 11, 1963, Alabama's governor, George Wallace, personally blocked the door to the admissions office at the University of Alabama to prevent black students from registering. In response, Kennedy authorized federal troops surrounding the building to force Wallace to step aside.

The next evening, June 12, Kennedy gave a nationally televised speech in which he said Americans could no longer ask blacks to "be content with . . . patience and delay." The president urged Congress to act on civil rights, but he presented no specific program.

Hours later, Medgar Evers, the leading NAACP official in Mississippi, was assassinated in the driveway of his home. The funeral of Evers, a World War II veteran and strong voice for civil rights, drew black and white political leaders from across the nation.

Kennedy Demands New Legislation

One week after Evers' death, Kennedy requested specific legislation from Congress to ban segregation of public facilities, strengthen the laws enforcing school integration, and offer greater federal protection of voting rights. Making this legislation come about would soon become the focus of the biggest peaceful demonstration the nation had ever seen.

Governor of Alabama George Wallace holds up his hand to Deputy U.S. Attorney Nicholas Katzenbach, who was trying to gain entrance for two African-American students to the University of Alabama. The widely publicized incident was one of several that persuaded President Kennedy it was time to act.

Chapter 3

Planning the March

In the view of march organizer Bayard Rustin, Philip Randolph was "the greatest leader of the twentieth century" in African-American civil rights. This photograph shows Randolph at the Lincoln Memorial on the day of the march.

Making the Decision

In the winter of 1962 to 1963, civil rights leaders began meeting to discuss a mass demonstration in support of their cause. Martin Luther King's assistants met with A. Philip Randolph, the civil rights leader who had pushed through civil rights legislation in the 1940s.

By June 1963, the SCLC had agreed to work with Randolph to plan a march in the summer of that year. The leader of the NAACP, Roy Wilkins, then pledged his support. In addition, white labor and church organizations offered their help. On June 11, Martin Luther King announced to the press plans for a march on Washington. The date was set for August 28, 1963.

On July 2, an organizational meeting for the march was held in New York City. It was the first time that the six leaders of the proposed march had met as a group. The march leaders were known as the "Big Six"—they were the public face of the march and gave it their support.

The Big Six

Asa Philip Randolph (1889–1979) pulled together a diverse group of civil rights activists to lead the March on Washington. As a prominent union leader and founder of the Negro American Labor Council, Randolph's focus for the march was to demand jobs for African Americans. **Martin Luther King, Jr.,** (1929–1968), the most famous civil rights leader of the 1960s, wanted to organize a protest that pushed for civil rights legislation. When Kennedy demanded action from Congress in June 1963, the legislation became an additional focus of the march. **Roy Wilkins** (1901–1981) led the NAACP from 1931 to 1977. He did not necessarily believe that protests were the best way to achieve civil rights, but he pledged his organization's support as long as the march abided by the law. After the march, Wilkins was influential in pushing for the 1964 Civil Rights Act. **James Farmer** (1920–1999), cofounder of CORE, was the organizer of the freedom rides that began in 1961. He later worked for the U.S. government in the Department of Health, Education, and Welfare. **John Lewis** (born 1940), a former freedom rider, was president of the Student Nonviolent Coordinating Committee from 1963 to 1966. He continued to be active in civil rights after the 1963 march. In 1986, Lewis was elected as a congressman from Georgia. **Whitney Young** (1921–1971) joined the National Urban League, an organization that protected the civil rights of minority groups, when he was a student. He was director of the league from 1961 to 1971 and, in that position, advised the federal government on poverty and other social issues throughout the 1960s and early 1970s.

The Big Six (from left to right): John Lewis, Whitney Young, Philip Randolph, Martin Luther King, Jr., James Farmer, and Roy Wilkins.

Bayard Rustin planned everything from the schedule of events to the efficient movement of huge numbers of people. Here, he explains a map to a group of volunteer marshals, whose job it would be to keep order among the marchers.

Behind the scenes, the planning was done by Bayard Rustin. He was known to be a brilliant organizer, and the entire occasion would have been impossible without his skills. Rustin had helped Randolph plan a similar protest march in 1941 that was eventually canceled. He had also helped King organize the Montgomery bus boycott and was one of the SCLC founders in 1957.

Getting Started

When the final decision to hold the march was made on July 2, Rustin had less than two months to organize the enormous event. Working day and night, he accomplished an extraordinary organizational feat. Within two weeks, he had printed and sent out two thousand copies of his Organizing Manual to civil rights offices across the nation to help each local group prepare.

The massive protest was named the "March on Washington for Jobs and Freedom." Although civil rights organizations had pledged money for the event, thousands of dollars still had to be raised. Rustin raised funds by selling march buttons for 25¢ apiece. By early

August, more than 175,000 march buttons had been sold, and 150,000 more were ordered.

Cooperation

Since the late 1800s, several large public protests had been held in the nation's capital. The 1963 march, however, differed in one important respect. President Kennedy, who had at first been doubtful, gave his support to the idea. This official approval led to a unique cooperation.

As Rustin and his assistants carefully worked out the plans, they were aware that anything other than a peaceful march would damage the cause of civil rights. The authorities, also, were determined to keep the protest nonviolent. Their common purpose meant that

At the march headquarters next to the Washington Monument on August 27, 1963, volunteers prepare signs for the march the next day. The signs were all red, white, and blue.

The Goals of the March

There were two main goals for the March on Washington: to get a meaningful civil rights bill—one that addressed housing, education, and voting rights—passed in Congress; and to demand a huge federal employment program for all working people, regardless of race. Other demands made by the marchers in 1963 included:
- the elimination of racial segregation in public schools;
- an end to police brutality at public demonstrations;
- a nationwide minimum wage of $2 an hour (at the time, it was $1 an hour);
- the enforcement of constitutional rights.

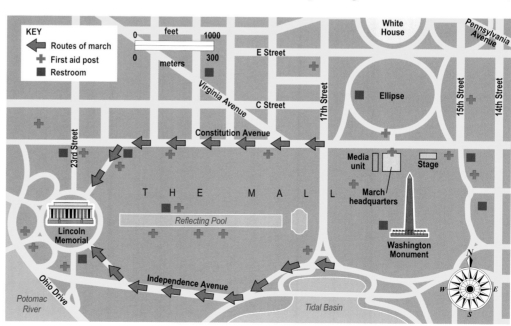
march organizers worked closely with government officials, the police, and other local authorities.

This cooperation was criticized on both sides of the political fence. Segregationists were horrified that the president would give approval to a protest against the government. **Radical** black activists, on the other hand, said that accepting support from the authorities would compromise the protest.

The organizers, however, were not trying to send their message to extremists on either side. They were trying to show Congress and the vast majority of people in the United States that the time had come for equal opportunity for all Americans, whatever their color.

Setting the Route

It was agreed that the march would originate at the Washington Monument, which stands in a large open area known as the Mall, south of the White House. After opening ceremonies there,

This map shows the area of the march and the official routes from the Washington Monument to the Lincoln Memorial. In fact, many people just walked straight down past the Reflecting Pool. Restrooms and first aid stations were dotted around the area.

marchers would walk west down either of two routes, Constitution Avenue or Independence Avenue, for about 1 mile (1.6 km). They would assemble again around the steps of the Lincoln Memorial —a symbol of freedom to all African Americans—to listen to the main speeches.

The authorities were largely in favor of the route of the march and the site of the speeches. This was mainly because the march would be in a limited area and therefore relatively easy to control.

Being Prepared

Steps were taken to ensure peace and order. All vacations for police officers were canceled for the day. The National Guard was mobilized, as were the local police reserve and firefighters. President Kennedy's administration added its security forces to supplement soldiers and police officers. Robert Kennedy, the president's brother and the U.S. attorney general, ordered police dogs to be kept completely away from the marchers.

The Justice Department and the police also worked with the march organizers on planning details. For instance, the government helped develop the most modern public address system possible, to allow all participants to hear any broadcast communication.

The march route kept people away from the White House and the Capitol (on the left in the background in this photograph). With the Potomac River running behind the Lincoln Memorial (front right), the crowd would have been contained had trouble broken out.

Chapter 4

A Day in Washington, D.C.

Marchers arrive at Union Station in Washington, D.C., on the morning of August 28, 1963.

Arriving in Washington

On August 28, 1963, New York City's 's Penn Station was packed with a huge early morning crowd boarding trains. Those people were just some of more than 200,000 Americans heading to Washington, D.C. Many had left weeks earlier. Members of one New York City chapter of CORE walked the 230 miles (370 km) to the march in just 13 days. A group of college students arrived after weeks of walking and hitchhiking 700 miles (1,126 km) from Alabama.

Trains and buses pulled into Washington's Union Station shortly after dawn. Many of the buses were chartered by local branches of the NAACP, SCLC, and other civil rights and labor groups. More than 30,000 marchers arrived in 21 chartered trains.

A Huge Crowd

Late summer in Washington, D.C., is a time of brutal heat and high humidity. The weather is so hot that the nation's capital seems almost empty. Residents often leave for vacations during that time. Many government offices shut down, and Congress is in recess.

August 28, 1963, however, was very different. Thousands upon thousands of people assembled on the slope beside the Washington

Monument to wait for the march to begin. The crowd was mostly black, but there were thousands of whites as well. Some were wealthy and famous, but most were ordinary working people.

With the Capitol building in the background, a stream of marchers heads to the Washington Monument for the first gathering.

When the Sun Came Up

"Somewhere between Baltimore and D.C. the sun began to come up. When you are in a bus like this at night you are in a closed world. You can't see what is around you. As the sun came up you see the whole freeway. All lanes completely jammed with buses. That's the moment we knew this march would be a big success."

Bruce Hartford, a student who took a bus from Connecticut, describing his journey to Washington, D.C.

The Morning Program

At the Washington Monument, a stage had been set up for the morning's entertainment. Shortly before 11:00 A.M., popular folk singer Joan Baez stepped to the microphone and sang two well-known songs of the civil rights movement: "Oh Freedom" and "We Shall Overcome." Baez was followed by more performers who sang

Fiery Words

Of all the speakers scheduled for August 28, none caused civil rights leaders more concern than John Lewis, leader of the SNCC. In the first draft of his speech, he compared civil rights workers to Union soldiers that destroyed the South under the leadership of General William Sherman at the end of the Civil War. His drafts declared,"We will pursue our own 'scorched earth' policy and burn Jim Crow to the ground nonviolently."

Almost everyone agreed that such words were too inflammatory, and Philip Randolph appealed to Lewis to tone down his words. Lewis had great respect for the longtime leader, and he made last-minute changes to the speech. Nevertheless, his anger was unmistakable when he criticized Kennedy: "This bill will not protect young children and old women from police dogs

John Lewis makes his controversial speech to a large crowd at the March on Washington.

and fire hoses when engaging in peaceful demonstrations. . . . Which side is the federal government on? Mr. Kennedy is trying to take the revolution out of the streets and put it in the courts. Listen, Mr. Kennedy, the black masses are on the march for jobs and for freedom, and . . . there won't be a 'cooling-off period.'"

folk songs and other popular songs of the time that focused on the themes of the civil rights movement.

As the music played on, the wave of people continued to walk from Union Station to the Washington Monument. When King, Wilkins, and Lewis left a meeting with congressional leaders and walked onto the steps of the Capitol, they were astonished at the number of people.

The March Begins

Although the march did not start officially until noon, thousands of people started walking shortly after 11:00 A.M. When the march leaders heard that the event had begun without them, they rushed from their meeting at the Capitol to join the crowd.

By mid-morning, the temperatures neared 90°F (32°C) and humidity hung like a blanket over the perspiring marchers. Many carried signs that addressed issues from labor to justice to civil rights. Hundreds of marchers from the United Auto Workers, a union that was one of the event's sponsors, held mass-produced signs such as, "UAW Says Jobs and Freedom for Every American."

Other marchers carried handmade signs. A young marcher carried a sign that read, "There Would Be More of Us Here But So Many of Us Are in Jail. Freedom Now." A woman carried a sign that

The event leaders lined up for the official start so it appeared they were at the head of the march. In fact, many impatient marchers had already set off.

Camera lights flare as Abraham Lincoln's looming statue looks down on the scene outside the Lincoln Memorial. Television cameras were positioned all over the Mall to broadcast the event to millions of people around the world.

demanded, "We Must Be Accorded Full Rights as Americans Not in the Future but Now."

At the Lincoln Memorial

News coverage for the event was larger than for any political demonstration in U.S. history. National newspapers and others from around the world had reporters on the scene. The three major U.S. television networks set up cameras around the Lincoln Memorial to broadcast the occasion. It was one of the first events ever shown live around the world by satellite.

By 2:00 P.M., the marchers had reached the Lincoln Memorial or the Reflecting Pool in front of it. The afternoon's events began with the national anthem and an opening prayer delivered by a Catholic leader from Washington.

Speeches, Prayers, and Songs

Philip Randolph then delivered the first speech of the afternoon. Randolph's speech was followed by remarks from a Protestant clergyman, which were followed in turn by a "Tribute to Negro Women Fighters for Freedom." Although no women spoke at the event, Bayard Rustin introduced six women, including Rosa Parks, who were applauded by the crowd.

Next came John Lewis, whose speech questioned the efforts of Kennedy and the federal government to bring about change. Of all the speeches, Lewis's stood out for the anger that many in the crowd felt about government inaction on civil rights. He was the only speaker to use the term "black." Most people at the time still used the term "colored" to refer to African Americans.

As the sweltering afternoon wore on, the president of the United Auto Workers spoke about economic equality. March leaders James Farmer, Whitney Young, and Roy Wilkins spoke. Between speeches, a church choir performed, a Jewish rabbi offered a prayer, and a famous gospel singer, Mahalia Jackson, performed inspirational songs that brought the huge crowd to its feet, cheering, clapping, and whistling.

Shortly before 5:00 P.M., as the relentless sun began to sink in the sky, Martin Luther King stepped to the microphone. King was widely considered to be the greatest speaker of the movement.

As temperatures rose, some demonstrators plunged their feet into the Reflecting Pool. The atmosphere at the march was friendly and peaceful.

On the stage in front of the Lincoln Memorial, King began his famous speech, "I am happy to join with you today in what will go down in history as the greatest demonstration for freedom in the history of our nation."

King then made a reference to Lincoln's most famous speech, the Gettysburg Address, which began "Fourscore and seven years ago." King said, "Fivescore years ago, a great American, in whose symbolic shadow we stand today, signed the Emancipation Proclamation." He praised Lincoln for ending slavery.

King said that black people remained slaves to discrimination. He warned that African Americans were no longer willing to wait for equality. His voice rose as he repeated phrases beginning with the word "now." "Now is the time to make real the promises of democracy; now is the time to rise from the dark and desolate valley of segregation to the sunlit path of racial justice; now is the time to lift our nation . . . to the solid rock of brotherhood. . . ."

King stirred the crowd as he delivered a blunt warning to those who opposed civil rights. He declared, "The whirlwinds of revolt will continue to shake the foundations of our nation until the bright day of justice emerges."

King reached the part of his speech that is so widely remembered: "I have a dream . . ." (King said later that he had not written those words in advance.) After an enthusiastic response to each "dream," King expressed another one, finally saying, "I have a dream my four little children will one day live in a nation where they will not be judged by the color of their skin but by the content of their character."

By this time, many people realized they were hearing one of the great speeches in U.S. history. The crowd roared when King concluded: "When we allow freedom to ring, when we let it ring from every village and every hamlet, from every state and every city, we will be able to speed up that day when all God's children, black men and white men, Jews and Gentiles, Protestants and Catholics, will be able to join hands and sing in the words of the old Negro spiritual: 'Free at last! Free at last! Thank God Almighty, we are free at last!'"

At Union Station, marchers wait to board trains for the journey home. The participants were probably aware that they had been part of a historic occasion.

The End of the March

The rally concluded as Rustin read out the goals of the march. His words were followed by a short prayer, and the crowd departed quickly and without incident. A cleanup squad of several hundred volunteers organized by Rustin made sure that every scrap of litter was picked up. As evening descended in the Mall, it was hard to imagine that thousands of people had so recently filled the area.

Greatest Day

"The March on Washington established visibility in this nation. It showed . . . that people were coming together. . . . It demonstrated that there was unity in the black community for the cause of freedom and justice. . . . I went back to the grounds about six or seven o'clock that evening. There was nothing but the wind blowing across the reflection pool, moving and blowing and keeping music. We were so proud that no violence had taken place that day. We were so pleased. . . . This was the greatest day of my life."

Ralph Abernathy, civil rights campaigner, quoted in Voices of Freedom
by Henry Hampton and Steve Fayer, 1990

A Meeting with the President

Those who participated in the march, as well as those who led it, were filled with excitement in the hours after the event. The Big Six and other civil rights leaders went directly from the Lincoln Memorial to the White House. There they hoped to develop a strategy with President Kennedy for passing the civil rights bill.

Yet, in a meeting that lasted slightly more than an hour, the civil rights leaders did not receive any direct promise of action from the president. While Kennedy personally admired the commitment behind the march, he still depended on southern Democrats in Congress for his political power. Kennedy refused to give the civil rights leaders a strong commitment of support.

Disappointment

The failure of the president and Congress to act quickly on civil rights caused some African Americans to feel betrayed. Many felt that the positive feelings generated by the march had helped the president, while he had done nothing to help the movement. The **militant** leader Malcolm X, who called for more aggressive action to achieve social justice, termed the event the "**Farce** on Washington."

Even the leaders of the march became disillusioned when the legislation on civil rights demanded by Kennedy in June 1963 was delayed. They wondered if they had compromised too much in order to ensure peace during the march.

A photo taken at the White House after the march shows (left to right): Whitney Young, Martin Luther King, John Lewis, Rabbi Joachim Prinz, Eugene Carson Blake, Philip Randolph, President John F. Kennedy, Walter Reuther, Vice President Lyndon B. Johnson, and Roy Wilkins.

New Voices of Protest

Bombing a Church

The violence toward blacks in the South continued. On September 15, 1963, slightly more than two weeks after the March on Washington, a bomb exploded in the basement of the Sixteenth Street Baptist Church in Birmingham, Alabama. Twenty-one children were injured, and four young girls died in the explosion.

Much of the nation was horrified by the bombing, and, in many ways, the event was a turning point in the civil rights struggle. From that point on, nonviolence lost its power to motivate many African Americans.

J. Edgar Hoover v. Civil Rights

FBI agents look for evidence outside the Sixteenth Street Baptist Church.

Throughout the 1960s, few federal government officials did more to undermine the civil rights movement than FBI director J. Edgar Hoover. On the morning of the 1963 march, Hoover ordered FBI agents to contact celebrities participating in the march to warn them that their careers would be ruined. Perhaps the worst marks against Hoover, however, were his actions after the Birmingham church bombing in September 1963, when his FBI agents were assigned to the investigation. Within two weeks of the bombing, agents had strong evidence against four men. Rather than arrest the suspects, however, Hoover ordered that the evidence be hidden. He claimed that civil rights activists had bombed the church themselves to gain public support for their cause.

The Civil Rights Act of 1964

On November 22, 1963, two months after the church bombing, President Kennedy was assassinated in Dallas, Texas, and Vice President Lyndon B. Johnson took office. In a speech to Congress the following week, Johnson called for lawmakers to pass a civil rights bill to honor the fallen president.

On July 2, 1964, Martin Luther King, Jr., stood near Johnson at the signing ceremony for the Civil Rights Act of 1964. The act prohibited racial discrimination in facilities such as hotels, amusement parks, and other public places. It protected voting rights and created the Equal Employment Opportunity Commission to assure the right to jobs. Finally, it gave the U.S. attorney general expanded powers to desegregate schools.

Enough Talking

"We have talked long enough in this country. We have talked for one hundred years or more. It is now time to write the next chapter—and to write it in the books of law."

President Lyndon B. Johnson in a speech to Congress, November 27, 1963

This photograph by James Kerales shows an important march that took place in Alabama in 1965. Protestors walked from Selma to Montgomery to demand voting rights legislation. They were harassed, beaten, and jailed, but 25,000 marchers still made it to Montgomery.

Voting Rights

Despite the broad reach of the Civil Rights Act, the South was unable to embrace racial equality. In August 1964, three civil rights workers—two white men and a black man—were kidnapped and

39

killed in Mississippi. A white woman working in voter registration was gunned down on a highway there as well.

Finally, in August 1965, President Johnson signed the Voting Rights Act, which allowed the federal government to oversee voter registration. The new act gave the vote to African Americans throughout the South for the first time since the 1870s. In spite of this step, however, poverty, unemployment, and poor housing caused race riots to flare in cities across the country.

King is Assassinated

On April 4, 1968, Martin Luther King was assassinated in Tennessee. The murder of the widely admired leader drained much of the energy from the peaceful side of the civil rights movement. In many ways, it marked the end of a remarkable period in history.

Other Protest Movements

A poster commemorating a Native American protest in 1973.

One legacy of the African-American civil rights movement is that it inspired other groups to protest for their rights. As early as 1961, a group of four hundred Native American leaders met to discuss their tribal rights and how to preserve their culture. In 1968, the Indian Civil Rights Act was passed, but Indians' demands for fair treatment continued for many years. Also in the 1960s, a growing, poverty-stricken Hispanic population found a voice for their protests in Cesar Chavez, leader of the United Farm Workers union. After Chavez organized boycotts and strikes in 1965, farmers who employed Hispanic agricultural workers were forced to offer better pay and working conditions. Meanwhile, women were feeling they, too, were being denied equal opportunity. In the late 1960s and 1970s, they campaigned for equal pay and education.

"Today you have a new generation of black people who have come on the scene, who have become disenchanted with the entire system, who have become disillusioned over the system, and who are ready now and willing to do something about it."
—Malcolm X—

The militant movement that emerged in the mid-1960s was called "Black Power." Militant activists, such as Malcolm X (center right), did not want to integrate but instead aimed to improve their own communities and raise African Americans' awareness of their roots and culture.

The Civil Rights Movement Changes

By the late 1960s, leaders of the traditional, nonviolent movement were considered too moderate by some activists. Young African Americans increasingly turned to organizations such as the Nation of Islam and the Black Panther Party. New, militant leaders, such as Malcolm X, Huey Newton, and Stokely Carmichael, called for violent resistance to racial prejudice and brutality. They said blacks should separate from whites instead of trying to integrate.

The new leaders appealed to African Americans to take pride in their history and heritage. They discarded the terms "Negro" and "colored" and used "African American" and "black" instead. Although these movements helped to achieve a cultural change in American society, they were less successful in achieving the political changes for which earlier leaders had hoped.

Conclusion

President George W. Bush lays a wreath at King's grave on Martin Luther King Day in January 2004. Coretta Scott King, the widow of the civil rights leader, watches.

A Beginning
"1963 is not an end, but a beginning."

Martin Luther King, Jr.

The March Remembered

The March on Washington is today generally remembered for King's dramatic speech, one of the great orations in history. Often over-looked is the contribution of the other civil rights leaders and the superhuman effort that was required to organize such a huge event in a period of less than two months. And, as it turned out, it was one of the best-organized and most peaceful demonstrations of its size ever held.

In the summer of 2003, the fortieth anniversary of the event, a memorial plaque was dedicated to the 1963 March on Washington at the Lincoln Memorial. Among those in attendance was Coretta Scott King, the widow of Martin Luther King, Jr. Also in attendance was the only surviving speaker from the 1963 march: John Lewis. Forty years later, the angry young leader of the SNCC in 1963 was a congressional representative from his home state of Georgia.

In the Bush administration that began in 2001, two leading U.S. officials were African Americans: Secretary of State Colin Powell and National Security Advisor Condoleezza Rice.

The Situation Today

Martin Luther King Day in January, when the civil rights leader is honored, has been declared a federal holiday. The struggles and legislation of the 1960s, together with later policies of **affirmative action**, have produced results. There are now record numbers of black elected officials across the country, and educational achievement among African Americans has improved.

Poverty, however, remains an enemy of minorities in the United States. Not only African Americans, but Hispanics and other ethnic groups, continue to earn less and hold fewer jobs of influence than white Americans. In spite of King's dream, the nation is still separated along racial lines.

The Legacy of the 1963 Civil Rights March

As successful as the March on Washington was as a political demonstration, there is disagreement about whether it led directly to political benefits for African Americans. Many historians believe that the bombing in Birmingham and the Kennedy assassination, two events that closely followed the march, played an even more important role in the passage of the Civil Rights Act. Many people, however, see the march as a special moment in the history of race relations in the United States. For them, it represents the highest achievement of the nonviolent civil rights movement of the early 1960s.

Time Line

1863	President Lincoln issues Emancipation Proclamation.
1865	Thirteenth Amendment is enacted.
1866	Fourteenth Amendment is passed by Congress.
1896	U.S. Supreme Court rules that "separate but equal" facilities are acceptable in *Plessy v. Ferguson*.
1909	National Association for the Advancement of Colored People is founded.
1941	President Roosevelt bans discrimination in the defense industry.
1942	Congress of Racial Equality is founded.
1948	President Truman bans discrimination in the military.
1954	U.S. Supreme Court outlaws school segregation in *Brown v. Board of Education of Topeka*.
1955	Montgomery bus boycott begins.
1956	U.S. Supreme Court outlaws segregation on buses.
1957	President Eisenhower sends federal troops to ensure school integration in Little Rock, Arkansas.
	Southern Christian Leadership Conference is founded.
1960	Sit-ins at lunch counter in Greensboro, North Carolina.
	Student Nonviolent Coordinating Committee is founded.
1961	Freedom rides begin.
1962	President Kennedy sends federal troops to the University of Mississippi to ensure integration.
	U.S. Supreme Court outlaws segregation of all public transportation.
1963	May: Police use fire hoses and dogs to attack civil rights marchers in Birmingham, Alabama.
	June 11: Alabama governor George Wallace blocks registration by black students at University of Alabama.
	June 13: Mississippi civil rights leader Medgar Evers is murdered.
	June 19: Kennedy requests civil rights legislation from Congress.
	August 28: March on Washington for Jobs and Freedom.
	September 15: Church bombing in Birmingham, Alabama.
	November 22: President Kennedy is assassinated.
1964	July 2: Civil Rights Act of 1964 is signed.
	August: Three civil rights workers are murdered in Mississippi.
1965	August: Voting Rights Act is signed.
1968	April 4: Martin Luther King, Jr., is assassinated.

Glossary

activist: person who takes action in support of or in protest against issues in his or her society.

affirmative action: action taken to improve opportunities for minorities.

Amendment: official change or addition made to the United States Constitution.

boycott: refuse to do business with a particular business in protest against its policies.

civil rights: basic rights—such as freedom of movement, property ownership, voting, education, and choice of religion and political beliefs—that every person should have.

demonstration: public show of beliefs or feelings by a group of people in support of a cause.

discrimination: showing preference for one thing over another. Racial discrimination happens when one racial group is given preference over another racial group.

emancipation: freeing of enslaved African Americans.

farce: something done just for show and not really meaningful.

federal: having to do with the whole nation rather than separate states.

integration: getting rid of segregation; the same as desegregation.

Jim Crow: fictional character of the 1800s created by a white performer to make fun of blacks. The name of the popular character was used to refer to segregation laws of the 1800s and 1900s.

legislation: process of deciding on and enacting laws; and laws that are enacted.

lynch: use a group of people unlawfully to attack and kill a victim.

militant: using aggression and sometimes even violence in campaigning for a cause.

naturalize: give someone the rights of citizenship.

racist: having opinions about a person based on his or her race rather than on his or her true qualities.

radical: very different or extreme.

segregation: separation of people of different races.

unconstitutional: action or law that goes against the principles of the U.S. Constitution.

union: organization that campaigns and negotiates for better working conditions for its members, who are usually workers from a particular trade or type of business.

voter registration: process by which a people's names are entered into local, state, or federal records so that they can exercise their right to vote in elections. Black people were discouraged by whites from registering to vote in the South, and civil rights activists worked to enable more African Americans to do so.

Further Information

Books

Allen, Zita. *Black Women Leaders of the Civil Rights Movement* (African-American Experience). Franklin Watts, 1996.

Hatt, Christine. *Martin Luther King, Jr.* (Judge for Yourself). World Alamanac, 2004.

McKissack, Frederick L. *This Generation of Americans: A Story of the Civil Rights Movement* (Jamestown's American Portraits). Jamestown, 2000.

Patterson, Lillie. *A. Philip Randolph: Messenger for the Masses* (Makers of America). Facts on File, 1995.

Wormser, Richard. *The Rise and Fall of Jim Crow*. St. Martin's, 2003.

Web Sites

www.civilrightsmuseum.org/gallery/movement.asp National Civil Rights Museum has online exhibitions about the struggle for civil rights since the time of slavery.

www.naacp.org Web site of the National Association for the Advancement of Colored People offers historical information and current news about African-American civil rights.

www.usinfo.state.gov/usa/civilrights Department of State web site honors the fortieth anniversary of the March on Washington with photographs, articles, documents, and many good links.

Useful Addresses

National Association for the Advancement of Colored People
4805 Mt. Hope Drive
Baltimore, MD 21215
Telephone: (410) 521-4939

Index

Page numbers in *italics* indicate maps and diagrams. Page numbers in **bold** indicate other illustrations.

African-American civil rights
    constitutional, 7, 14, 25, 32
    legislation for, 9, 11, 21, 22, 23, 25,
       30, 37, 39, 40, 43
    movement, 5, **10**, 12, 13, 14, 16–20,
       21, 22, 23, 31, 37, 38, 40, 41, **41**, 43
    organizations, 9, **9**, 10, 11, 12, 13, 16,
       18, **18**, 19, **19**, 21, 22, 23, 24, 28, 30,
       41, 42
    protests, 4, 16, 17, **17**, 18, **18**, 19, 20,
       20, 21, 22, 23, 25, 30, **39**
    see also March on Washington
    and voting and voting rights
Alabama, 13, 16, **16**, 20, **21**, 28, **39**

Baez, Joan, 30
Baker, Ella, 16
Big Six, the, 22, 23, **23**, 37, **37**
Birmingham, 13, 16, 18, 19, 20, **20**, 38,
    38, 39, 43
Brown v. Board of Education of Topeka, 14

Carmichael, Stokely, 41
churches, 9, 16, 17, 22, 38, **38**, 39
Civil Rights Act of 1964, 23, 39, 43
Congress, 7, 11, 20, 21, 23, 25, 26, 28,
    37, 38
Congress of Racial Equality, **18**, 19, **19**,
    23, 28

Du Bois, W. E. B., 9

Eisenhower, Dwight, 15
Emancipation Proclamation, 5, 6, 34
employment, 10, 11, 12, 23, 25, 30, 31
    discrimination in, 12, 13, 39, 40, 43
Evers, Medgar, 21

Farmer, James, **19**, 23, **23**, 33
Faubus, Orval, 15
Fourteenth Amendment, 7
freedom rides, 19, 23

Gandhi, Mahatma, 18
government, U.S., 11, 23, 25, 27, 28,
    and civil rights, 5, 6, 11, 12, 13, 21,
       30, 32, 38, 40
    see also Congress
Greensboro, 17, **17**

Hoover, J. Edgar, 38

Jackson, Mahalia, 33
Jim Crow, *see* segregation
Johnson, Lyndon B., **37**, 39, 40

Kennedy, John F., 19, 20, 21, 23, 25, 26,
    27, 30, 32, 37, **37**, 39, 43
Kennedy, Robert, 27
King, Coretta Scott, 42, **42**
King, Martin Luther, Jr., 16, **16**, 24,18, 22,
    23, **23**, 39, 40, 42, **42**, 43
    at March on Washington, 4, 33, 34–35,
       34, 37
Ku Klux Klan, 7, **7**, 10

labor unions, 12, 22, 23, 28, 31, 33, 40
Lewis, John, 23, **23**, 30, **30**, 33, **37**, 42
Lincoln, Abraham, 5, **5**, 6, **22**, **32**, 34
Lincoln Memorial, 4, 5, **5**, **22**, 26, 26, 27,
    27, 32, **32**, 34, 37, 42
Little Rock Central High, 15, **15**
lynching, 8, 9, 10, **11**

Malcolm X, 37, 41, **41**
March on Washington for Jobs and
    Freedom, **4**, 19, **22**, 26, 38, 42
    goals of, 4, 23, 25, 36
    importance of, 4, 36, 37, 43

leaders, 22, 23, **23**, 30, 30, 31, **31**, 33, 37, **37**
marchers, 4, **4**, 5, 26, 28, **28**, 29, **29**, 31, **31**, 32, **32**, 33, **33**, 34, **34**, 35, **35**, 36, **36**, 37
media coverage, 4, 32, **32**, 33
orderly and peaceful nature of, 4, 25, 33, 36, 37, 42
organization of, 24, **24**, 25, 26, 27, 36, 42
plans for, 22, 23, **23**, 24, 25, 26, 27,
signs at, **25**, 31–32
size of, 4, 21, 28, 29, 31, 36, 42
speeches at, 4, 30, **30**, 32, 33, 34–35, 42
Mississippi, **18**, 40
Montgomery, 19, 39
bus boycott, 16, **16**, 24

National Association for the Advancement of Colored People, 9, **9**, 11, **11**, 13, 16, 21, 22, 23, 28
National Urban League, 23
Negro American Labor Council, 23
New Deal, 11, **12**,
New York City, 10, **10**, **11**, 22, **23**, 28
Newton, Huey, 41

Parks, Rosa, 16, 32
Plessy v. Ferguson, 14

Randolph, Asa Philip, 12, 13, 22, **22**, 23, **23**, 26, 30, 32, **37**,
Reflecting Pool, **5**, 26, 32, **33**
Robinson, Jackie, 13
Roosevelt, Franklin D., 11, 12
Rustin, Bayard, 16, 19, 22, 24, **24**, 25, 32, 36

segregation and desegregation, 5, 8, **8**, 9, 10, 12, 12, 17, 20, 21, 30, 34, 39
in education, 8, 14, **14**, 15, **15**, 20, **21**, 39

of transportation, 8, 16, **16**, 19
sit-ins, 17, **17**
slavery and slaves, 5, 6, 7, 8, 34
South, the, 5, 10, 13, 17, 30, 40
racism in, 6, 7, 8, 9, 10, 14, 39
state and local governments, 6, 8, 9, 11, 15, 16
violence in, 7, **7**, 10, 11, 16, 18, 19, **20**, 21, 38, **38**, 39, 40
see also segregation
Southern Christian Leadership Conference, 16, 19, 22, 24, 28
southern states, *see* South, the
Student Nonviolent Coordinating Committee, 18, **18**, 23, 30, 42

Thirteenth Amendment, 6, 7
Truman, Harry S., 13

Union Station, 28, **28**, 31, **36**
United States, 6, 7, 12, 26, 43
military forces, 6, 13, **13**, 15, **15**, 20, 21, 27
see also government, U.S.
United States Supreme Court, 14, 15, 16, 19

voting and voting rights, 8, 9, 13, 21, 25, 39, 40
see also African-American civil rights
Voting Rights Act, 40

Wallace, George, 20, **21**
Washington, D.C., 4, **6**, **7**, 19, 25, 26, 28, **28**, 29, 32
Washington Monument, **4**, 26, 26, **27**, 28–29, 30, 31
White House, the, 26, 26, 37, **37**
Wilkins, Roy, 22, 23, **23**, 33, **37**
World War I, 10, 13
World War II, 12–13, **13**, 21

Young, Whitney, 23, **23**, 33, **37**